AF392420

MICHAEL DANIELS

The Story
I Tell Myself

Discovering the true narrative of my life

BITÁCORA DEL ESCRITOR
PUBLISHING HOUSE

The story I tell myself:
Discovering the true narrative of my life

By Michael Daniels

DR © 2024 Michael Daniels

Cover Edition: Bitácora del Escritor
Proofreading: Theö Stamper
Panama City, Panama
ISBN: 978-9962-8596-5-9

First edition 2024

Dedicatory

This book is for you, who got tired of pretending to be strong. For you, who swallowed your tears, who adapted so much that you didn't even know who you were anymore. I dedicate it to you without sweet words, because you've had enough of that already. I dedicate it to you if you ever thought you were the problem, when in reality you were just surviving with the little you were given.

It's for you, who were brave but no one noticed. For you, who loved from the wound, who gave more than you had, who waited for someone to come and save you, not knowing that you were the only one who could do it.

This book is not for those who want to seem healthy. It's for those who want to be real. For those who are tired of repeating the same story. For those who feel alone amidst the noise. For those who stay silent a lot, but inside have a fire that is begging to come out.

I dedicate this to you if you're ready to stop hiding, to look at what hurts without blinking, to live barefoot and with your soul exposed. This book won't give you answers. It's going to make you uncomfortable until you tell yourself the truth.

And if it hurt, it's because you were ready.

Index

Preface

What if what you tell yourself isn't true?

I don't know how many times I've told myself the same story. Sometimes without meaning to. Sometimes as a defense. And other times, with such conviction, that I swore it was true.

But there's something curious about what we tell ourselves when we're alone. That internal voice that no one else hears. That which is not shouted, but defines what you decide. The one that doesn't write on paper, but ends up marking the path of your entire life. I want you to be honest for a moment: Have you ever stopped to really listen to it? Not what you say out loud. Not what you post on social media, nor what you repeat in front of the mirror. But rather what you tell yourself when no one is watching. Because that's where it all begins. In that silent story. In that whisper disguised as certainty.

I also lived like that once. One day I found myself walking through a life that seemed like mine, but it wasn't entirely. It was like living inside a suit that someone else had sewn: it covered me, but it was tight. I was living a script that I hadn't written.

And not because I hadn't had my own experiences. But because many of those experiences were loaded with what others thought it should be. What they expected from me. What was supposed to be "the right thing." And what I thought I had to accept to not break.

But something inside broke anyway. And that's where everything started to change. It wasn't magical. It wasn't quick. It was strange, painful, brutal, uncomfortable, and necessary. And it's that when you start to question your own narrative, you find yourself naked in front of your history.

And that, my friend… that hurts. But it also liberates. That's why I'm here. That's why you're reading this. Not to give you formulas. Not to tell you how you should live. Not to preach from a place where everything is already resolved.

I'm here to talk to you. To have a conversation that isn't about me, but inevitably carries my voice. A conversation where the only thing that matters is that you listen to yourself beyond the noise.

This book has no pretensions. It has wounds. Has discoveries. It has truths that I didn't always want to accept, but now I understand that I needed to look at. It's not a guide. It's a meeting. Between you and you. This isn't about erasing your history. It's about seeing which parts no longer represent you, and having the courage to write new ones, even if your hand trembles.

And yes, it's difficult. But it's also powerful. Because we are not just characters in this life. We are the authors. And if we don't like how the current chapter is unfolding, we have the option and the responsibility to write another one.

So here's the only question that really matters: Are you going to keep telling the same old story, or are you going to dare to write the one you really want to live?

Introduction

Each Have you ever felt it? That silent story that runs inside. That story you didn't consciously write, but still repeat. That script that no one handed to you, but you still know it by heart.

We all carry one. It's that invisible narrative woven between memories, beliefs, unspoken wounds, and desires. It's a voice inside us that doesn't ask for permission to decide who you are and how far you go. And the most curious thing is that we almost never question it. We live from there. From that story that was being written when you still didn't know you were writing it. From those inherited phrases, those learned gestures, those silences you interpreted in your own way. I realized it late. Or rather, I realized just in time. I discovered that there were parts of me that weren't mine. Stories I told myself because it was easier to believe them than to dismantle them. And the truth hurt me. Not because they were completely false, but because they no longer represented me. They had become outdated. They had expired. But I kept acting as if they were my only option.

And that's when I sat down with myself. And I can tell you that it wasn't a comfortable talk. It was a conversation where I finally dared to say things to myself that I had avoided for years.

This book was born from that. Not as a "self-help manual," but as an uncomfortable and necessary conversation between you and you. I'm just here to accompany you, to throw questions at you that don't have easy answers.

To walk with you while you unearth truths you already knew, but had buried under layers of habit. I'm not going to tell you how to live. I'm not that kind of voice. If it's your decision, I just want you to dare to look at your history head-on, without embellishments. I want you to ask yourself just one question:

"Am I living my story... or the one they told me I should live?"

If the answer stirs you, then you are exactly where you need to be. Let me tell you this right away. I'm not looking to change you. The only thing I'm interested in is returning the pen to you. So that you, with your own words, can start writing what you truly want to be. Because it is possible. It's tough, it's painful, but in the end, it's the most beautiful thing you'll do for yourself and for those who truly see you.

And you know what? Start now. Now. Right here.

CHAPTER 1

THE POWER OF INTERNAL NARRATIVE

The story you tell yourself defines the life you live.

Sometimes, when you are in silence, when there is no one around you, when you don't have to act or pretend, that voice appears. It doesn't shout, it doesn't need to. He knows you too well. That voice is you, or at least the version of you that you believed in

We all carry a narrator within us. A private narrator who has been with us since before we had words to name what we felt. And that narrator is not neutral. He has his style, his fears, his reasons, and he has the habit of telling you who you are, even if you are no longer that person.

That's where it all begins. Not in what happens to you, but in how you tell it to yourself. That internal narrative is more powerful than any external influence, because it not only interprets reality, it constructs it.

If you keep telling yourself that you're not enough, you'll act as if you aren't. If you tell yourself that you are always abandoned, you will create the conditions for it to happen again. If you believe you don't deserve more, you'll settle for what hurts less

And you'll do it without even realizing it.

That's the messed up thing about the internal narrative: it feels so familiar that you confuse habit with truth.

Now you're not here to repeat the script. You're here just to question it. And no, you don't need to break everything all at once.

Sometimes, all it takes is one sincere question: "Is what I'm telling myself true? Or is it just what I've always told myself?" That question opens doors.

When you start to observe your history from a distance, you discover things. You discover that many phrases you repeat are not yours. That there are ideas installed by someone else. That there are beliefs inherited out of fear, not out of truth. That you're playing a role that no longer fits the person you're trying to be.

So, here's the important part: Your internal narrative is not a reflection. It's a construction. And like any construction, it can be redesigned.

Not with empty phrases or social media claims. But with presence, discomfort, and absolute honesty.

The first thing required to write a new story is to have the courage to read the one you have already written and decide, clearly, which parts you no longer want to keep repeating.

Origin of our stories

Have you ever wondered when it all began? Not what you lived, but what you believed about what you lived. It's just that what happened is not the same as the dramatic movie you told yourself afterward.

Most of the things you believe about yourself today didn't come from a conscious decision. They were planted. Like phrases that someone else threw into the air and you, unknowingly, caught with your soul.

"That's not for you."

"You are too sensitive."

"You need to try harder."

"You're not going to get anywhere like that."

Most of the time, it wasn't what they said to you, but what they didn't say. A silence, an absence, a hug that never came, or a disapproving look.

And you, little one, interpreted. Because human beings need meaning. And since you didn't have all the information, you did what you could: you filled the gaps with your imagination and started writing.

From there, your story was born. And no, it wasn't a fair story. It was a story pieced together with fragments, with bits of what you understood, with wounds you turned into rules, and with moments that shaped your identity.

And do you know what's the strongest part? That story is still alive today.

Even though you're no longer five years old and you may have healed many things and tell yourself that "you've already gotten over everything." I invite you to go back, but not to get stuck.

But just to understand again. Because if you don't see where the story you're telling yourself today began, you'll keep acting from an old script, one you didn't write consciously.

And there's something you need to hear clearly: The origin does not define you, but if you don't know it, it controls you. You are not condemned to be who you were when you were afraid, nor are you trapped in the interpretation of that moment. You can go back, look with new eyes, and realize that many of those conclusions are no longer true.

You're in time. Not to erase what has been lived, but to rewrite what it means to you today. That is your power.

Influence of the environment

Sometimes we believe we are free. That everything we think, say, or feel comes from an authentic, clean, personal place. But if you stop for a second, if you breathe and look closely, you realize that not everything you believe about yourself is truly yours.

There are things that stuck to you without warning. Like the accent you mimic as a child, the phrases you hear so often that you end up repeating them without thinking, or that feeling that something is wrong with you, but you don't know exactly where it came from.

The environment is not just the place where you grow up. It's the sum of all the invisible messages that taught you how you're supposed to be. Your family, your street, the school, the church, the television, the adults who spoke to you and those who didn't.

All of that shaped you. It gave you codes, it taught you what was good or bad, even if no one explained it to you. He taught you who deserved affection, and who did not. Who had value. Who was dangerous. And who had to stay silent to avoid causing discomfort.

And you, like any child, just wanted to belong. So you accepted, assimilated, and molded yourself. You swallowed many ideas without digesting them, because there was no other option. Because questioning them was too dangerous when you needed love to survive.

But now you're no longer a child. Now you can stop. You can observe which part of your narrative comes from your voice and which part is an echo of an environment that no longer represents you.

Do you really think you can't?

Or did someone teach you to believe that and you just followed the script?

Are you really clumsy with emotions?

Or did no one ever give you space to express them without shame?

Do you really not have enough worth?

Or were you raised in a system that measured worth with rules that never included you?

The environment has power. But it's not eternal. Today you can decide what to keep, what to let go, and what you need to relearn from a healthier place.

The role of the subconscious

Tell me something, Have you ever done something and not understood why you did it? Have you ever felt a reaction come out of you without warning, without logic, without permission? I promise you, you're not crazy. You are just inhabited by layers of yourself that you don't know are there, but they are. Directing, editing, and choosing for you when you think you are choosing.

That which we call the subconscious is neither a closed box nor an esoteric cloud. It's a deep archive of everything you couldn't process at the time. Everything that hurt and went unspoken, what you didn't understand and assumed anyway, what you lived in silence, interpreted with fear, and kept without questioning.

It's there. And even if you don't see it, it acts. He is the ghostwriter who makes you distrust love even though you say you're looking for it, the one who tells you that you can't when you're about to attempt something big, the one who triggers fear just when you're about to open up, and the one who whispers old stories when you're already trying to write new ones.

He doesn't do it out of malice. He does it because his job is to protect you. And he does it from what he knows. Even if that knowledge is based on broken experiences, outdated rules, and wounds that should no longer have a voice.

That's why you repeat.

That's why you sabotage yourself.

That's why sometimes you don't move forward even if you want to. Because there's a part of you that still believes it's dangerous to move forward.

And that part is hidden, not absent. Denying it doesn't make it disappear. Looking at it does transform it.

This is not a call to fight with your subconscious. It's an invitation to listen to it from another place. To ask yourself with humility:

"Is what I'm feeling real or just an echo of something unresolved?"

That's where all the magic begins. Not in controlling everything. But in illuminating what previously acted from the shadows.

When you make the unconscious conscious, you regain control of your story. You no longer act from who you were. You act from what you now understand you can be. The subconscious is not an enemy. It's your guardian. But he needs you to teach him new ways to take care of you. And that, my brother, only you can do.

Narrative as a defense mechanism

I'm going to tell you something that was hard for me to accept: not everything he told me was true. But somehow it served and protected me.

The internal narrative doesn't always seek the truth. Sometimes it just seeks to hurt less, and that's why we use it as a shield, as an elegant, well-justified barrier, to avoid having to look at what we are still not ready to feel.

And it works. Yes, it works. It gives you meaning, relief, and a reason that sounds coherent to explain what you don't want to see with brutal honesty.

"It wasn't meant for me."

"That's just how I am."

"It's just that I have bad luck."

"They don't understand me."

"I always give more, and they let me down."

Does that sound familiar to you? To me, yes. Those phrases are not just thoughts. They are walls. Small emotional bricks that we place to avoid feeling naked in front of our wounds.

It's that accepting that we were part of the mistake, that we chose from fear, that we stayed where we knew we were fading away, that... that hurts more than any comfortable narrative. So, what do we do? We create a version of the facts where we come out clean. Where everything has a logic that doesn't compromise us. Where the other person was the toxic one, fate was unfair, life let us down.

And pay attention here, it's not about pointing fingers or blaming you. It's about awakening.

Every time you tell yourself a story to avoid an emotion, you are also avoiding a part of yourself that needs to be heard. Narrative as defense has its moment. Sometimes we need it to avoid breaking. But if it becomes your usual way of interpreting life, then it no longer cares for you: it limits you. It doesn't tell you the truth; it tells you what you want to hear, and that sounds nice until you realize you're going in circles.

So here comes the question that makes those hidden emotions bleed:

What magical story are you telling yourself now to avoid feeling what you really feel?

Because there is the door. In that story that sounds convincing, but no longer makes sense with your present. When you have the courage to look beyond the protective narrative, you will find a truth that not only hurts but also liberates.

And that one is definitely worth writing.

Narrative turned into reality

What you are experiencing today is not just a consequence of what happened. It is also, and often above all, the result of what you told yourself about what happened.

There is a very fine line between thinking something and living as if it were absolute truth. So fine that you don't even realize when you cross it.

Everything starts with an internal phrase, a feeling, a brief anecdote.

"I'm not enough."

"This always happens to me."

"I don't deserve anything better."

"I can't trust."

"The same thing always happens to me."

And at first, it's just a thought. But then you repeat it to yourself. And you repeat it. And you behave from there. And you start making decisions as if that story were real. And without realizing it, you turn it into your experience.

And that's not a coincidence. It's coherence. Your mind seeks for everything to fit with what you believe. So, you filter, interpret, and select experiences that confirm your narrative. The rest you ignore, invalidate, and sabotage.

Have you had a good opportunity and let it pass without knowing why? Did you distance yourself from someone who actually wanted to stay with you without even realizing it? Did you postpone something you wanted with all your might?

That wasn't a coincidence. That was an internal story acting from the shadows. And you didn't do it because you're weak. Rather, you did it because there was a script behind it.

One that said: "This is not for me." One that you were taught or that you yourself wrote from an old experience, but that no longer applies.

The narrative turned into reality is neither magic nor a mystical law. It's emotional logic. You believe something enough and end up behaving as if it were true.

And so, what was just an idea... becomes your day-to-day life. In your relationship, in your bank account, in your body, in your level of faith, and in your way of loving or hiding.

That's why it's so important to pay attention to what you're telling yourself inside. Not to punish yourself. But to regain control. Because if you can create a reality from a story that doesn't serve you, you can also create a new one from one that does illuminate you.

The question is no longer: *Why is this happening to me?*

The honest question is: *What story am I telling myself that makes this keep happening?*

And that answer could change everything.

CHAPTER 2
CHILDHOOD AND THE ROOTS OF THE STORY

Childhood plants the roots of the stories we carry within us.

You didn't choose your childhood, no one does. You were born in a place with certain people in an emotional, social, and spiritual context, and you simply adapted. You didn't know what was fair or unfair, you didn't know if you were getting too much or too little. You only knew that this was life and that, somehow, you had to survive it.

That's where your story began. Not with words, but with sensations, with glances, with hugs given or denied, with voices that shaped you and silences that did too. Childhood is not just a stage. It's the base code. It's the emotional software on which you later installed everything else. And if that code has errors of love, presence, recognition, they will inevitably replicate, over and over again, until someone corrects them.

That someone... is you.

What you learned back then, when you didn't have tools, might not be useful to you today. But you keep using it. You keep operating from those old learnings. From those beliefs that were formed when all you wanted was not to lose affection. When crying was wrong or making a mistake was dangerous and being yourself didn't guarantee acceptance.

That's where many of the stories you tell yourself today were born. And even though years have passed, they remain active. Like internal alarms that go off when someone gets too close. Like patterns that repeat in your relationships. Like reactions you don't understand, but can't avoid.

No, you're not damaged. You're programmed. And the good news is that the programming can be updated. But first, you have to have the courage to look at the roots. Without judging them. Without romanticizing them. Just look at them.

This is not to relive childhood from the pain. It's to recover the emotional truth that got trapped there. And from that truth, start writing a new story where you are no longer the child who survives, but the adult who decides.

First impressions

Tell me: do you remember your first emotional wound? That moment when something broke inside and no one noticed?

Probably not. Because it wasn't an obvious trauma. It was something small, almost imperceptible. But it was etched in. A poorly spoken word. An absence that hurt more than it should have. A gesture that made you feel invisible. A "don't do that" that not only corrected your behavior but also planted the idea that there was something wrong with you.

That's how first impressions are born, not the ones you have of the world, but the ones the world imprints on you when you still have no defenses. And those impressions, those soft but definitive marks, become internal molds, the first chapters of your personal story, a story you didn't consciously write, but that today defines you without you knowing it.

Maybe someone yelled at you once, and you learned that raising your voice is normal. Maybe someone left, and you understood that love always abandons. Maybe you tried to show your emotion and they laughed, and since then you decided to hide what you feel to avoid being embarrassed again.

The problem is not what happened. The true impact lies in how you interpreted it. Because when we are children, we don't have the tools to filter. We absorb everything as truth. And everything that is repeated becomes identity.

Thus, without realizing it, you started to see yourself as they treated you. You started to think that you deserved what you got. You started to act from a version of yourself that didn't come from your soul, but from your need to fit in.

But listen to me carefully: that version is not you. It's just the first impression. And first impressions can also be questioned, can be understood, can be rewritten.

This moment is your opportunity not to judge the past, but to reclaim the right to narrate yourself from a fairer place. The next time you react without understanding why, ask yourself: Did I learn this… or did I really choose it?

That's where the change begins. That's where your real story begins.

Family influence

There are things they didn't tell you with words, but they still left a mark. And almost everything you believe about yourself today started there: in that nucleus called family.

You might think that your childhood was normal. But that word, in my experience, is dangerous, because sometimes we normalize abandonment, comparison, the shout disguised as correction, the silence used as punishment, or the demand as a form of love.

And there you were, trying to understand the world through the eyes of those who raised you and trusting blindly, because you had no other choice.

At that moment, your family was your universe. And if something didn't fit, you didn't think: "this is wrong." You thought:

"It must be my fault."

"I am the problem."

"I have to change so that they love me."

"That's how love is shown."

And that narrative, that way of interpreting what you lived, became your truth. A truth that you continue to carry today and most likely without being aware of it.

Sometimes, the way you talk to yourself is a perfect replica of how you were spoken to as a child. Sometimes, the way you relate to others is an exact copy of what you saw between your parents. Sometimes, your soft boundaries or rigid walls don't stem from your character but from a family system that unintentionally trained you emotionally.

But here's the hardest part: they were also raised by someone. This is not about blame, it's about cycles. Of patterns that repeat, unconscious loyalties, and unspoken mandates that still govern you from within.

"Don't talk about what you feel."

"Be strong."

"Men don't cry."

"Women have to endure."

"Don't be a problem."

"Don't be like your father."

"Don't disappoint me."

Phrases like those are not just heard, they are tattooed on the soul. And after all this time, you still react as if you were still trying to earn that love, that approval, that place. But you don't have to do it anymore. Today you can look at your family history with compassion and firmness, recognize what they gave you, but also see what was missing. And from there, decide what you keep and what you let go.

It's not about renouncing your roots. It's about healing what grew crooked. So that your tree doesn't repeat the same curves. So that the story you write today no longer has to hurt the same way.

The social and cultural environment

You were born into a world that already had rules. Before you had consciousness, a mold was already waiting for you. You didn't create it. You just arrived and started to adapt. The social environment didn't ask you who you wanted to be. It showed you who you were supposed to be. It taught you how to speak, how to dress, how to behave, how to love, how to express yourself, how to be a man or a woman, how to fit in without bothering anyone.

And you, with that soft and open heart, did what any human being needs to do: belong.

And to belong, sometimes you had to disappear parts of yourself. Be silent when you wanted to scream, smile when you were broken, adjust when all you wanted was to be free.

The environment wasn't always cruel, but it was constant. And the constant shapes you, gets you used to it, convinces you, trains you to interpret the world from a framework that wasn't necessarily yours.

Society has its own narrative, and that narrative, if you don't question it, becomes yours.

"Success looks like this."

"A happy family behaves like this."

"You can't fail."

"Your worth depends on what you achieve."

"You always have to be strong."

"If you don't meet the standard, you're broken."

And you, wanting to feel normal, started narrating yourself from that lens. You pushed yourself, you compared yourself, you measured yourself against foreign scales, you distanced yourself from who you were to get closer to who you were supposed to be.

And maybe today, even with achievements, even with recognition, you feel empty. Do you know why? Because you are playing a character that does not stem from your truth, but from social conditioning. But listen to this:

culture cannot define you if you don't allow it. The environment can influence you, but it cannot possess you. You are free to question what you inherited. To break away from what doesn't resonate with you. Of reconstructing your identity without asking for permission. Sometimes, the greatest act of self-love is disobeying the world's expectations to obey your soul.

The personal myths of childhood

When you're a child, you don't understand the world, you just feel it. And what you can't understand with logic, you complete with imagination.

That's what children do: they create myths, internal stories, invisible explanations, and tailored truths so that the heart doesn't break.

And I don't mean fairy tales. I mean the ones you didn't tell anyone about. Those that were born in silence, but became the foundation.

"If I try really hard, they will love me."

"I shouldn't bother anyone with my problems."

"I always have to be strong."

"Love hurts, but it's normal."

"If I'm good, they won't abandon me."

"If I make a mistake, they will reject me."

"I have to do everything perfectly so they notice me."

Those weren't thoughts. It was emotional survival. Your soul needed to understand why something hurt, why someone was missing, why love was unstable, why you, being so much you, weren't enough.

And since there were no answers, you created them.

Do you see?

Those myths didn't arise from the truth, but from necessity. And that's okay. Because at that moment, they protected you. They gave you structure. They gave you a way to navigate the world without collapsing. But today you are no longer that child. Today you can look at them from another place. And that's where it hurts. Because part of healing is recognizing that many of the things you tell yourself today come from a wounded child trying to make sense of things.

And no, you're not weak for still believing them. You are human. But now you are a conscious human, and that changes everything.

This is the moment to review those myths. Not to destroy them with anger, but to look at them with love and say: "Thank you for protecting me, I no longer need you."

Because yes, you can rewrite the story. A story where you don't have to earn love. Where you don't have to carry everything. Where you can fail and still be worthy. A story not dictated by a confused child but by an awakened adult.

The persistence of children's narrative

What if I told you that many of your decisions today are being made by a seven-year-old version of you? It sounds ridiculous, but it's real.

The body grows, language evolves, responsibilities change, but there is a part of you that got stuck in an old story. And when that story was not healed, it continues to function as if time had not passed. As if you were still the same child who felt unchosen, who wasn't enough, who had to take care of everything to not lose love.

And it's that child who appears every time you feel rejected. Every time you compare yourself. Every time you feel like they're going to leave you, even though no one has said it. Every time you can't set a boundary without feeling guilty. Every time you sabotage yourself just before achieving it. Every time you choose from fear.

That childish narrative persists because you haven't updated it. Because you etched it in stone during a vulnerable moment, and then life confirmed it for you so many times that you no longer questioned it.

I'll tell you something that will probably make you a bit uncomfortable. The fact that something repeats doesn't mean it's really true, it just means you haven't faced it with a fresh perspective. And that new perspective is something only you can give yourself. And it's because you're no longer in that house, you're no longer that age, you no longer depend on that love to exist, and now you can choose.

But first, you have to identify which story keeps running in the background. The one that says you must endure, the one that makes you believe that love is always about sacrifice, the one that convinces you that if you speak up, you will annoy, the one that silences your intuition because it's not the right time, or the one that still waits for someone to come and save you. You know which one it is. Because it hurts every time it activates and because you recognize it, even if you don't always know how to deactivate it.

Today, it's not about denying your inner child. It's about taking it out of the driver's seat.

Tell him or her:

"Thank you for protecting me when no one else did."

But now I'm here. And I'll take care of it.
That's rewriting. That's real growth.

CHAPTER 3
THE HEROES AND VILLAINS OF OUR HISTORY

The heroes and villains of our history are reflections of our own internal battles.

Every story needs characters. But what no one told you is that those characters weren't always real. Some of them you created yourself, from what you needed to believe to survive.

And no matter how old you are, you still live your life reacting to them. Your hero can be that idealized version of yourself: strong, right, impeccable, without mistakes. That one who never cries, who always solves everything, and who "should be able to" even though they are crumbling inside.

On the other hand, your villain can be that part of you that you doubt, the one who makes mistakes, the one who stays silent when they should speak, the one who didn't know how to protect you in time, the one who loved poorly, or the one who failed.

Villains can also take the form of others: your absent father, your controlling mother, that person who made you feel small when you needed validation the most. And this curiosity will make you laugh: sometimes your hero and your villain are the same person. The one you love and hate at the same time. The one who marked your history, but also messed it up.

And you.

You keep writing your script as if that story had never been closed. As if you still had to prove something to the hero. Or unconsciously take revenge on the villain. But this is the plain and simple truth: no one, absolutely no one, has as much power over you as the version you yourself constructed of that person.

Now that's good news. Because if you created that internal narrative, you can also reconstruct it. And no.

It's not about erasing what happened. It's about understanding from where you continue to act. Because sometimes, you keep fighting battles that no longer exist. And you're defending yourself against enemies that only live in your memory and imagination. Ask yourself:

What would happen if you let go of the hero? What if you stopped demanding perfection from yourself? What if you could fail and still be worthy? What if you accepted that you don't need to rescue anyone?

What if you embraced the villain? Not the one who hurt you, but that part of you that you used as an excuse to not move forward. The part you have judged, but that just wanted to be seen.

This is not to idealize or to blame. It's to recognize who are inhabiting your internal story. And see if it's time to give them another role or, simply, close their chapter. I'll conclude with this: your true freedom lies not in creating new characters, but in stopping the fight with the old ones.

Identifying heroes and villains

Be silent for a moment.

Close your eyes and think: Who was that person who marked your history for better or for worse?

Shhh…

Don't strain to justify, don't try to make it rational, just feel.

Deep down, you already know who your hero was. But you also know who played the role of the villain in your life.

And sometimes, it hurts to accept it. Because sometimes the hero wasn't who they were supposed to be. And the villain didn't always have bad intentions. But the impact... the emotional impact, that was real.

Your hero might have been that aunt who listened to you when everyone else silenced you, or that teacher who saw you when you couldn't see yourself. It could have been that friend who didn't let you go when you were falling apart, or maybe even a figure you built in your head because no real person protected you as you needed.

And the villain... the villain can be harder to name. Because sometimes you loved him. Sometimes he took care of you and hurt you at the same time. Sometimes it was your own reflection. That part of you that you abandoned to fit in. That internal voice you learned to repeat after hearing it so many times outside.

I don't want you to identify them to judge. Rather, it's to locate. To understand from where you are living today. Because as long as you don't know who occupies those places in your internal narrative, you'll keep acting from a script that doesn't fully belong to you.

And be careful here, because sometimes, out of loyalty, you keep defending the hero, even if it means betraying yourself. And out of fear, you keep running from the villain, even though they no longer have power over you.

I propose this real exercise to you: Look at your current relationships, your decisions, and how you talk to yourself when you fail.

There they are. They continue to influence, camouflaged in your thoughts, reincarnating in every opportunity you don't take or in every affection you reject before being rejected.

Name them.

Not to give them power. But to reclaim it for yourself. Identifying your heroes and villains is the first step to writing a story where you are the protagonist and not the supporting character of their actions.

The impact of heroes on our self-image

Heroes not only inspire, they also condition. The problem was never admiring them; the problem was comparing yourself to them.

Since childhood, we seek role models. Someone who shows us how to be, how to survive, how to belong. And when we find that someone, real or imaginary, we imprint their image in our minds and start to evaluate ourselves by that standard.

"I want to be like him."

"I have to be strong like her."

"If I'm not like that, I'm not enough."

And without realizing it, we stopped being ourselves. We started to build an idealized version, based on what we admired, on what seemed right, and on what others applauded.

And that's where the self-image fragments.

Every time we don't reach that figure, every time we feel we fail to resemble that hero, we feel we fail as people.

And it's not just about distant idols. Sometimes your hero was your mom, your brother, or your spiritual leader. That person who seemed to have everything figured out.

And you, feeling incomplete, made their image a goal and yours a debt.

The problem is that no one is perfect. Not even heroes. But when you put them on a pedestal, you place yourself below. And that distance fills you with judgment, shame, and silent pressure. It makes you feel like you're always missing something. That no matter how much you progress, you still don't arrive.

But, where to? To whom? To what standard are you trying to conform?

Write this in your narrative: if your self-image is born from the reflection of another, it will never be enough.

Because you are not recognizing your own greatness, but imitating someone else's.

It's time to break the hero's mirror. Not to destroy it, but rather to stop measuring your worth from there. Your story deserves to be written with your voice, your face, your scars, and your image. Your real image, without filters, without masks, is worth more than any idol you tried to resemble.

The question is not: Am I living up to my hero? The question now is: Am I being fair to myself by continuing to believe that I have to resemble someone else to feel worthy?

Confronting your inner villains

Do you know who has hurt you the most in this life? You. And you know it.

Not because you wanted to, but because they never taught you to look at yourself without fear. And what is not looked at transforms into shadow. In parts of you that you hide, repress, deny. But they still act. And they act really strongly.

Those are your internal villains. They don't come with a cape nor do they have a voice from the grave.

But they do have your tone, your face, your words, your way of sabotaging yourself just before achieving something, your way of abandoning yourself every time someone else rejects you, your way of demanding perfection from yourself to feel worthy, and your way of punishing yourself for feeling.

And the worst part is that, many times, you don't even realize you're doing it. You only feel tiredness, self-hatred, doubts, and that emptiness that neither success, sex, nor recognition can fill.

Because you're not fighting with the outside world, you're fighting with yourself. And that fight is unfair because you yourself created those villains. They didn't come into being on their own. You gave birth to them in moments of pain, humiliation, and abandonment.

And you let them grow because they made you feel like they were protecting you.

"Don't feel, because feeling makes you weak."

"Don't trust, because trusting breaks you."

"Don't dream, because failing hurts more."

"Don't show who you are, because no one stays."

That's the voice of your villain. But that voice was once your shield. What happens is that what protected you as a child is now imprisoning you as an adult.

So yes, I have to tell you: you're going to have to confront them. But not like someone who is going to destroy them, but like someone who is going to sit down with them, look them in the eyes, and say:

"I no longer need you to survive." Now I can choose how to live.

The inner villain is not defeated by shouting. It is defeated with presence, truth, boundaries, and fierce compassion.

And yes, it's going to hurt a lot. Your ego is going to shake like you can't imagine. Your inner child is going to cry like never before.

But later… later you will be able to talk to yourself differently. From a self that does not betray itself. From a new story that is not written by fear, but by dignity.

Transforming conflict narratives

There are conflicts that do not arise from the other. They are born from you. From the story you already have written before the other arrives. And that's why, sometimes, unintentionally, you provoke the same ending even if the character changes.

Why?

Because it's not about what's happening now. It's about what you haven't resolved yet. And it's that every conflict you experience carries your voice within, your unresolved pain, your need to be right, and your terror of feeling like that again. And then, you act to protect yourself, but you end up repeating the same story.

You react before you listen. You attack before feeling. You shut down before trusting. And all of that is written from an internal narrative that says:

"They are going to betray me."

"I am worthless."

"I have to defend myself."

"I always end up losing."

"If I don't control, they crush me."

"If I don't anticipate, they hurt me."

That wasn't said by the person in front of you. You said it, years ago. And you keep living it as if it were a prophecy you need to prove.

So, how is a conflict narrative transformed?

It's not with diplomacy or techniques. It's with radical honesty.

First, you have to ask yourself a question that no one wants to ask: "What emotional benefit am I getting from holding onto this conflict?"

Maybe it gives you identity.

Maybe it makes you feel strong.

Maybe it allows you to continue being a victim. Or maybe you just don't know how to relate without drama, because you never learned any other way.

Whatever you believe makes sense. But it no longer has to be your truth.

Transforming a narrative of conflict doesn't mean pretending to be at peace. It means reviewing from where you are entering the battle. And if that place is old, painful, inherited, then maybe you no longer need to fight. Maybe you just need to change the story you're defending. And right there you start to have power over your story and you look at yourself without excuses. And you start to choose instead of react, and finally see that you can end a war that was never yours, because you understood that it was just taught to you.

The role of anti-heroes

Not all the people who impacted your story can be clearly classified. There are those who came into your life and gave you something while taking something else away. And that's why they hurt differently.

That's an antihero. Someone who saved you from something, but also broke you. Maybe it was a father who provided, but didn't know how to love. A mother who took care of you, but forgot to look at you. A teacher who pushed you, but never acknowledged you. A love that made you feel alive, but also drained your soul.

These people don't fit into extremes.

And there's the problem: because the mind wants clarity, but the heart remembers contradictions.

And then you don't know whether to miss them or resent them. You don't know whether to thank them or let them go. And the hardest part: you don't know if you can talk about what hurt you because there was also something good.

That's how antiheroes work: they teach you to live with emotional ambiguity. And if you don't recognize them, if you don't name them for what they were, you fill yourself with guilt for feeling what you feel.

And that guilt transforms into silence. And that silence into internal conflict. And that narrative conflict that you drag into all your current relationships.

Without realizing it, you keep trying to redeem the antihero or become one yourself. The one who does good, but puts themselves last. The one who takes care of everyone but doesn't take care of themselves. The one who holds up, even when no one holds them up. The antihero also lives in you. And sometimes you use it as armor.

But you don't have to do it anymore. The true act of emotional maturity is accepting that someone left a mark on you without having to idolize or destroy them. You can keep what they gave you and leave behind what they took from you. You can thank the push and close the wound. You can remember without attachment, without myth, and without debt.

And there begins your freedom and the start of a new narrative.

CHAPTER 4
THE WOUNDS HIDDEN IN OUR WORDS

The wounds hidden in our words are scars that only the soul can see.

Wounds don't always bleed. Some hide behind a phrase said with coldness. Of a joke thrown with venom disguised as humor. Of an "everything's fine" that hides storms. From an "I don't need anyone" that actually pleads, "Can someone stay?"

Yes, words have an edge. And what we say sometimes is just a smokescreen to avoid showing what we still don't know how to heal.

When a wound is not attended to, it's a discourse. And that discourse becomes a habit. And that habit becomes identity.

Then you start to speak from your pain without realizing it. To relate from fear disguised as pride. To establish connections where words build walls, when what you want most is for someone to tear them down.

How many times did you use irony to avoid crying? How many times did you speak harshly so they wouldn't notice how fragile you were? How many times did you stay silent about what hurt you and end up exploding over something that had nothing to do with it?

Each word is a clue. Each conversation is a mirror. Each reaction is a poorly translated emotional scream.

This is not about judging you. It's about stopping. To ask yourself this question naked and with total honesty:

From where am I speaking? From the anger you don't recognize? From the disappointment you never verbalized? From the feeling that if you show your vulnerability, you'll lose?

Your emotional language is full of clues. And if you give yourself permission to observe it, you will find there the wounds that it's time to face head-on.

Not to dramatize or to victimize yourself. But to truly heal. When you heal what you kept silent, you no longer need to shout for them to hear you. Nor hide behind phrases that don't identify your truth.

Your way of speaking can be your prison or your freedom.

This is an invitation to listen to yourself like never before, to stop using words as a shield and start using them as a bridge.

Towards yourself.

Towards others.

Towards a story where speaking is an act of presence, not of defense.

Recognizing the invisible wound

There are wounds that are not visible. They don't bleed, they don't make noise, and they have no witnesses. But they accompany you every day like an echo that won't be silenced.

They wake you up in the way you doubt yourself. In the way you find it hard to trust. In that contained anger that explodes over trivial things. In the constant effort to prove your worth, even though deep down you're not convinced of it.

The invisible wound is the one that wears you down the most. Because it is not recognized by others, nor by yourself. You pretend to be strong, you keep yourself busy, you push through, and without realizing it, your whole life turns into a kind of emotional armor. A suit that fits you tightly, but that you no longer know how to take off without feeling naked in front of yourself.

And do you know what makes it so dangerous? That since she doesn't scream, no one asks if you're okay.

And since no one asks, you learned to say nothing. Sometimes, the invisible wound is born in childhood, when you needed to be seen and they made you feel like you were too much or not enough. Or simply invisible.

Other times it is born from a betrayal, from a breakup you couldn't process, or from a word someone said that you believed forever. And since there was no visible drama, the story remained archived but never closed.

Today you continue walking with it. And every relationship, every project, every attempt is affected by that silent burden that you don't know how to name.

But here you are.

And finally, you're asking yourself: What part of me is hurting that I haven't wanted to see? What wound am I covering with productivity, with distance, with sarcasm, with control?

Recognizing the invisible wound doesn't make you weak; rather, it makes you free. Because once you see it, you can decide what to do with it and stop acting as if it weren't there. You can choose to either heal it, talk about it, or embrace it, and you don't need to fall apart. You just need to stop pretending it doesn't hurt.

The language of pain

Pain speaks. Not always with shouts, sometimes with long silences, with curt responses, with an evasive look, or with a "never mind" that actually means "please, stay."

We all develop our own language of pain. We do it from childhood, when we feel something so big that we don't know how to express it, and the body, the mind, and the emotions seek another way to release it without collapsing.

And so a gesture, an attitude, and a pattern become a habit.

There are those who express it through anger because it's easier to explode than to accept that they are broken inside.

Others show it with indifference because if they don't feel, they don't risk being hurt again.

There are those who become complacent, who laugh at everything, who never inconvenience anyone, because they learned that "if I'm good, they won't abandon me."

And there are those who become controlling because they feel that if they don't have control, everything will fall apart.

That is the language of pain. The one you developed without realizing it. The one you still talk about every time someone touches an open wound. The one you even use on yourself when you repeat harsh phrases, when you sabotage yourself, when you abandon yourself emotionally.

And the saddest part of all is that no one notices. Because pain isn't always visible. But it is always transmitted.

And if you don't become aware of how you're communicating it, you'll keep creating relationships based on a conversation that the other person doesn't understand and you don't know how to stop repeating. Today, I invite you to listen to yourself differently and ask yourself:

"What am I trying to say every time I shut down?"

"What part of me is seeking attention when I react like this?"

"What phrase couldn't I say... and it became my way of being in the world?"

Recognizing the language of pain is not falling into eternal sadness. It's translating the soul. It's giving voice to what was previously only expressed with reactions, with distance, with masks.

And when you manage to translate yourself, when you can say, "This hurts me" without fear, then your bonds stop being battlefields and become spaces of truth.

Narratives of self-pity and victimization

There comes a point on the journey where pain starts to define you. And without realizing it, you go from being someone who was hurt to becoming the person who always suffers, the one who never makes it, the one who is always left behind, ignored, and betrayed. An eternal victim of their circumstances.

And of course it hurts. Of course, there were real stories, traumas, absences, losses, unheard screams, and hugs that never came. Of course, you cried alone more than once.

But there comes a point where the pain stops being a memory and becomes a structure. In the way of living, as an excuse not to change, and as a justification not to take risks.

"It's just that I'm like this because no one supported me."

"I don't trust because I've been let down before."

"I don't open up because they always end up hurting me."

"I am not cut out for this; I never could."

"I give my all, and no one appreciates me."

They're not confessions. They are chains that you yourself are holding. And this is where misunderstood self-pity comes in. That which is not tenderness, but self-deception.

That which doesn't embrace you but rather lulls you to sleep.

It makes you feel that it's okay to stay in the same place because you've already suffered too much.

Poor thing. Read and reread the following.

One thing is having been a victim, and something very different is choosing to continue being one.

And yes, it may sound harsh. But it's also the exit door. Because as long as you keep telling the story from the place of "I couldn't, I don't matter, or I don't deserve," you will continue attracting situations that confirm that version of you.

And you are not made to live in a wound. You are made to heal it and transcend it. To tell another story. One where you were indeed hurt, but you didn't stay broken. One where there was darkness, but you learned to light your own way.

Breaking the narrative of victimization does not mean denying the pain. It means stopping using it as your calling card. And start narrating yourself from the power you have today, not from the absence you experienced yesterday.

Healing through rewriting

Rewriting is not denying what happened; it's stopping the painful repetition.

There is a huge difference between remembering your story and reliving it every day without realizing it. Many live with an old script stuck to their chest. One that says you can't. That you've already tried it. That it's not for you. That if you showed your soul once and they broke it, now you must always hide it.

No… You are not obligated to keep performing that play. Rewriting doesn't happen with words; it happens with decisions. With a new perspective. With a boundary you didn't know how to set before. With a conversation where you finally say what you never dared to. With a different response to that old stimulus that used to dominate you.

Healing through rewriting is looking in the mirror and saying, This did hurt me, and it did leave a mark. But I no longer want to live conditioned by this. Today I write something new even though my voice still trembles.

Writing from the soul is choosing truth, even if it still hurts a bit. Choose freedom, even if at first you feel dizzy.

And you don't need to have everything figured out to do it. You just need to be willing to stop telling yourself the same story with the same endings.

The paper is no longer written; the ink is yours. And if you've learned anything up to this point, it's that it doesn't matter how your story began; what matters is how you decide to end it.

CHAPTER 5
REWRITING THE SCRIPT

By rewriting the script, we reinvent the story we want to live.

There is a brutal moment when you wake up. Not because everything is clear, but because something inside you can no longer bear to stay the same. That's where the rewriting begins.

It's not like they portray it in self-help books. It's not a blank slate, a new version, or a list of affirmations stuck on the mirror. It's looking at your history, just as it is, with its stains, its gaps, its contradictions, and saying: up to this point, others wrote it. From now on, I write it.

Rewriting is not erasing the previous one. It's deciding the perspective from which you're going to tell it. You can narrate your life as an endless tragedy or as a journey of resilience, awareness, and transformation.

The difference is not in what happened. It's in how you choose to tell it. And even more: how you choose to act from now on. This chapter is a declaration of emotional independence. A permission to challenge the beliefs you swore were true. A break from the excuses that sound logical but keep you trapped. I'll repeat them to you again:

"That's just how I am."

"It always happens to me."

"It's just that no one in my family ever changes."

"I wasn't born for that."

"I can't handle it."

"I can't handle this."

All of that are lines from an old script. And you know what? You can stop repeating it.

The moment is now. The day is today. Not because you're ready. But because you're already fed up with telling yourself the same thing. And when you get fed up, you start writing differently. And even if you still don't know how the story ends, you've already started to change it.

Limiting narratives

The limiting narrative is that repeated whisper that became structure. A simple phrase, an inherited idea, or a poorly digested interpretation that now guides your decisions, your fears, and your resignations.

And the worst part of it all is that it sounds logical. Sounds like yours. It sounds so familiar that you don't even question it.

"I'm not good at that."

"It's too late."

"That's not for me."

"I wasn't born with that talent."

"I always find it harder."

"I don't have what it takes."

You wear them as if they were your skin. You repeat them without realizing it. And the worst part is that you defend them.

Now it makes sense for us to do it, because acknowledging that you are limiting yourself would mean accepting that the obstacle is not outside. It's inside.

And, obviously, that is indeed scary.

Because, what do you do when you discover that you are the one with the chain tied to your ankle? The first thing is to understand something key: your limiting narrative didn't originate with you. They planted it in you, and then you watered it innocently.

Maybe someone told you that as a child. Maybe you saw it at home. Maybe it was a painful experience that you associated with failure and closed off forever. But the fact that the story is old doesn't mean it has to continue being true.

Every time you repeat a limiting narrative, you give it more strength. More power. More shape. And without realizing it, you live to confirm what you fear the most.

Today you're here to interrupt that cycle. To ask you just one question that shakes everything: What if what you always believed is no longer real?

What would change if you let go of the idea that you can't?

Who would you be without the story of not being enough?

What doors would you knock on if you didn't feel ashamed of failing?

Limiting narratives are not eliminated with nice phrases. They crumble with action. With a different decision. With a "yes" where you used to say "I can't."

With a step forward, even if everything trembles.

What limits you is not the world. It's the voice in your head saying you're not ready, that it's not for you, that you've already tried. That voice can turn down the volume. But you have to tell him: "Thank you for protecting me, but you are no longer the one writing my story."

The rewriting process

Although I already talked to you about rewriting, I want to delve a bit deeper into it here. As you already know, rewriting is not starting over. It's daring to look at what you've already written and not run away.

It's sitting down in front of the emotional text of your life, underlining the parts that no longer resonate with you, crossing out what doesn't represent you, and telling yourself, with guts, with ovaries, and with truth:

"This is no longer me."

Record this: the true rewriting process doesn't start with what you want to achieve.

It starts with what you are no longer willing to keep holding on to.

And there, right there, is the uncomfortable and messed up part. Because it implies recognizing that you told yourself stories that worked for you for a while but now suffocate you.

"I have to prove."

"There's always something missing."

"I must please."

"If I show myself, they reject me."

"That's just who I am; I can't change."

Each of those phrases may have made sense at some point. Maybe they protected you and somehow helped you survive.

But living is not the same as surviving.

Rewriting is not erasing your past. It's redirecting your present with awareness. It's asking yourself: From what place am I acting today? From the self that was hurt or from the self that wants to heal? What part of me needs to keep believing that love is not for me? Since when did I start believing that if I try, I won't be able to achieve what I want?

And I reaffirm it to you. The process hurts. Because when you truly rewrite, you're not changing yourself; you're recovering yourself. You reconnect with parts of yourself that you hid. With dreams that you buried. With truths you hid to fit in. And when you see them, when you bring them back, the story changes on its own.

You no longer walk like someone begging for love.

Walk like someone who loves themselves enough not to lie anymore.

And yes, there are relapses. Days when the old narrative wants to come back. Days when your body doubts. Days when you get tired. But on those days, remember this: Every word you choose to think, say, or remain silent about is another line in the new script of your life.

You are not obligated to repeat the same ending. You can let go of the character you no longer are. And write, finally, like someone who recognizes themselves as whole even amidst the chaos.

Change the focus

There are moments when what you need is not a new beginning, but a new approach. The story can remain the same. The past doesn't change, the events happened, the pain was real, and the losses were too.

But you change when you decide to look at all that from another perspective. And that's where the alchemy happens. Not magical, rather human and brave.

Changing the focus doesn't mean sweetening what hurt. It's not about covering up what broke you with pretty phrases. It's understanding that the same event that once destroyed you can today give you direction.

What you once saw as abandonment can now be space to return to yourself.

What you felt as betrayal might be the sign that it was time to let go of bonds that no longer honored you.

What you read as failure might be the door forcing you to create something of your own, something authentic, something without permission.

The focus changes everything. Where you once saw limitation, now you see choice. Where there was once only lack, you start to see possibilities. And where there was only fear, a new question finally appears: What if this didn't happen to me, but for me?

That question doesn't justify everything, but it does give you back your power. Because you can't change what was, but you can decide from which place you tell it, use it, honor it.

Changing the focus is opening your eyes without anesthesia. It's taking what has been lived and saying: this is also part of me. But it won't be the part that holds me back. It will be the part that grounds me. And from there I grow.

Rewriting exercise

Before you start, breathe. Close your eyes for a moment. Don't focus on "doing it right," but on being brutally honest.

This exercise is not to correct you, but rather to acknowledge you. And from there, choose differently.

Take several blank sheets or a notebook and write.

Part 1: The narrative that limits you today.

Write without filters. Without trying to sound good.

Just you with yourself. Start with this phrase and let it flow: "The story I've been telling myself so far says that…"

Let it out.

Just as it comes.

Hurt. Repeated. Unfair. Immature.

It doesn't matter. Take it out.

When you're done, read it.

Out loud, if you can.

And look at it for what it is: a mental construct, not an absolute truth.

Part 2: What that narrative has caused

Now write this:

"By living from that story, I have denied myself…"

And be specific.

Father. Mother. Siblings. Friends. Loves. Projects. Freedoms. Real commitments.

What have you left out of your life by continuing to believe that story?

Here begins the change.

Because what you recognize, you can transform.

Part 3: What you do want to share from now on.

Now, yes.

Rewrite.

From the skin.

From the decision.

From the hunger to live differently.

"The story I choose to tell about myself from today is…"

And it doesn't matter if it's not perfect.

It matters that it is born from your current truth, not from your wounded past.

Make it yours.

With your words.

In your tone.

Not to please anyone.

Just to go back home… to you.

This is not done just once. This exercise is a ritual that you can repeat every time an old story tries to pull you back. And if you do it for real, if you do it with intention, you will discover that what changed was not just the story. The protagonist changed. You changed.

The impact of a new history

There comes a moment when you stop waiting for something to change outside and understand that everything changes when you change the story from within. It's not a nice phrase. It's a hard, transformative, and permanent truth.

When your narrative changes, you act differently. You no longer accept what you used to tolerate. You no longer bend for crumbs. You no longer justify what used to destroy you. You no longer ask for permission to be who you really are.

Your language sharpens. Your gaze becomes clearer. Your decisions are more yours. Your boundaries no longer sound aggressive; they sound like self-respect.

And all of that comes from a single source: the story you now tell yourself. The new story doesn't erase your past. It recontextualizes it. It turns it into building material.

Where there was once trauma, now there is transformation. Where there was abandonment, now there is strength. Where there was fear, now there is direction.

And maybe life didn't become perfect. But yes, more yours, more real, and more honest.

The impact of a new story is evident in your relationships, in your body, in how you sleep, in how you talk to yourself in the mirror, and in how you no longer seek validation where you once begged for love.

A new narrative is not a change of script. It's a change of soul. And when that happens, things around you also start to fall into place.

Not because the world has changed. But because you no longer relate from emptiness. Now you do it from the root.

CHAPTER 6

THE IMPORTANCE OF LISTENING TO OUR OWN VOICE

The voice that really matters is the one you hear

in the silence of your soul.

There is a silence that weighs more than any scream. That one that echoes inside when you disconnect from yourself. When you got used to living according to what others expected. When you acted out of inertia, out of necessity, out of habit, and stopped asking yourself: "Do I want this, or am I just repeating it?"

Listening to your own voice is not something that is done with the ears. It's done with presence. Because your voice doesn't shout. Whispers. And if you have too much noise in your head—noise of judgments, of shoulds, of inherited fears—you won't hear it.

You got lost when you stopped asking yourself how you felt. You numbed yourself when you started to please others. You dimmed when you adapted your life to fit in instead of daring to embody your truth.

And now you realize: every transformation begins when you return to yourself.

Listening to your own voice is recovering that broken compass. That one that got buried under phrases like

"You are always so dramatic."

"That's not realistic."

"You're too old for that."

"And what if it goes wrong?"

"It's not that big of a deal."

"Don't be selfish."

All those foreign phrases, you made them yours. And along the way, you silenced the only voice that knew who you really were.

Today, this chapter doesn't ask you to have answers. It asks you to be silent. So you can hear what never stopped being there.

The voice that asks you to rest. The one that pushes you to stop begging for love. The one who reminds you that that project isn't crazy. The one who speaks softly to you when you punish yourself. The one who shouts "Enough!" when you can't take it anymore.

That voice is you. And it doesn't come back by force. She returns when you call her with respect.

Listening to you is an act of radical self-love. One that doesn't need approval. One that doesn't follow trends. One that doesn't shout: "Look at me." One that says: "I have myself."

When you regain your voice, you no longer sell yourself for crumbs. You no longer betray yourself to avoid discomfort. You no longer need the world to tell you who you are.

You know it, and you hold it. Even if everything shakes.

Distinguishing the inner voice

There are many voices talking to you at the same time. Some sound like your parents. Others like teachers. Or like your exes. Some come disguised as logic. Others out of fear. And a few more of social expectations that you never questioned.

So… How to distinguish your inner voice?

Keep this in mind: the inner voice doesn't shout, doesn't push you, doesn't punish you, doesn't negotiate from guilt. The inner voice guides you to the truth, even if it hurts. It confronts you with love, even if it's not what you want to hear. It speaks to you from within, not from duty. That voice that tells you "do it even if you're scared" is not anxiety; it's intuition. The one that whispers to you,

"This is not the way, even if it seems perfect," is not sabotage; it's wisdom.

But to hear it, you need silence. And I don't mean turning off the music or stopping looking at your phone. I mean silencing the voice that demands you to be someone else. Silence the voice that compares you. That belittles you. That repeats what you were told and turned into law.

Take the test:

Close your eyes.

Ask yourself: "What do I need right now?"

Wait.

Don't analyze.

Just listen.

The first voice will be the ego: fast, reactive, controlling.

The second one, the one that speaks softly, without hurry… that's it.

That's your inner voice. And when you recognize it, everything changes. You no longer convince yourself with excuses. You no longer manipulate yourself with fear. You no longer need external approval to move forward.

Because you finally know how you really sound. And that's the beginning of a brutal freedom.

The impact of external noise

We live surrounded by noise. But not the kind that is measured in decibels. But rather that subtle, constant, emotional noise that pushes you to be someone you're not without even raising your voice.

External noise doesn't always sound like shouting. Sometimes it sounds like advice you didn't ask for. To opinions that cut through you like blades. To expectations that settled in without you realizing. To comparisons disguised as motivation.

"And when are you getting married?"

"Don't you have kids yet?"

"You should be more like..."

"At your age, you should already have..."

"That doesn't make you money."

"That's not stable."

"That's not normal."

And you, in the midst of all that, trying to listen to yourself, trying not to fade away, and trying not to betray yourself.

But it's difficult. Because when the external noise is louder than your inner voice, you end up living on autopilot. You chose a career because it was what was expected. You stayed in a relationship because "it doesn't look good to break up." You kept your ideas to yourself because "it's not the right time." You kept your essence out of fear of being a bother.

And that noise becomes normal. So normal... that you no longer distinguish it. But you feel it. In the exhaustion that won't go away, in the insomnia, in the silent frustration, in that feeling of being full on the outside but empty on the inside.

Today, you don't have to fight against the world; just for a moment, lower the volume outside to raise the volume inside.

That means you're going to have to choose, filter, distance yourself, set boundaries. And yes, sometimes disappoint. But I prefer to disappoint the world than to keep denying myself.

Living under external noise is like dancing to a song you don't like just because everyone is applauding.

Turn off the noise. Listen to yourself. And listen to yourself. Not because it's easy, but because it's the only thing that really matters.

Cultivating authenticity

Authenticity is not about showing yourself as you are on social media, nor about being transparent because it's trendy. It's about daring to be yourself, even when you don't fit in. Even when they don't applaud you. Even when your knees are shaking.

And cultivating that, my dear reader, is a daily act of courage. Because the easy thing is to adapt. Become the version that people like. The one who doesn't make others uncomfortable. The one who knows when to stay silent, smile, and pretend that everything is fine. The easy thing is to be accepted. The brave thing is to be real.

Being authentic doesn't mean "doing whatever I want." It means doing what honors me, even if others don't like it. And that cultivation begins with the simplest and most fucked-up thing at the same time: telling you the truth.

Not the embellished one. Not the one that sounds good in public. Yours.

What hurts you? What no longer represents you? What do you do out of habit and not out of conviction? What are you holding onto just out of fear of being alone? Cultivating authenticity means facing that head-on and not running away. It's staying with yourself even if you don't understand everything, even if you're not perfect, even if you're still in process.

And little by little, you realize something beautiful: that when you stop imitating, you start inspiring. That when you stop lying to yourself, your body relaxes. That when you choose from your truth, life aligns itself.

No, it's not always comfortable. But it's yours. And that's enough. Because you didn't come to this life to pretend to be someone else. You came to embody your truth, even if it hurts, even if it brings you to tears, even if it leaves you alone for a while.

Authenticity is not inherited. It is cultivated with presence, with silence, with decisions that feel coherent even if they don't look pretty.

And when you start living like that, you stop searching for peace, because you become it.

Living in harmony with our history

Rewriting is an act of awareness. Living in harmony with what you wrote is an act of coherence.

Many manage to see themselves from a new narrative. They can express it in words, even write it with dazzling clarity. But when looking at their lives, they continue acting from the previous version.

"I know my worth... but I keep choosing relationships where I'm not seen."

"I know I deserve freedom... but I don't allow myself to change anything."

"I know I have power... but I keep hiding behind fear."

Real harmony occurs when what you think, what you say, and what you do resonate in the same tone.

And that is felt. In the way you talk to yourself. In the decisions you no longer postpone. In the relationships you no longer tolerate. In the no that you used to fear saying and now you express with firmness.

Living in tune with your story is not betraying what you discovered. It's telling yourself: If I already know who I am, then I have the responsibility to honor it in my day-to-day life. It's not about perfection. It's about presence. There are days when you'll stray from the path, when you'll act on autopilot, when the old fear will want to return.

But now you can no longer play dumb, because you've already listened to yourself, you've already seen yourself, and you've already written down who you are. And that, even if it's uncomfortable, can no longer be unseen.

Living in harmony with your story is not a destination. It's a daily practice. Like someone who looks in the mirror and reminds themselves:

"Today I choose myself too."

"Today I also stand by my truth."

"Today I also act like someone who knows their worth."

And if one day you forget, turn back the page, read your new story, and return to yourself.

At the end of the day, when you live from your truth, there is no external noise that can throw you off your center.

CHAPTER 7

THE IMPACT OF SELF-NARRATIVE ON RELATIONSHIPS

How you tell your story defines how you connect with others.

Your relationships are not broken. What is sometimes broken is what you believe you deserve within them. If you tell yourself that you are insufficient, you will seek to prove your worth over and over again. And you'll end up choosing people who only know how to love you if you prove something to them.

If you make an effort.

If you adapt.

If you break.

If you narrate yourself as "the one who always disappoints," you're going to distrust even when everything is fine.

You're going to sabotage.

To wait for them to abandon you and, unwittingly, you will provoke the abandonment you feared.

If your story says that "you can't count on anyone," you'll never let go completely. You will never let anyone take care of you. And even if you say you want love, you'll close the door before it knocks.

Your personal narrative is the emotional script from which you relate to others. And without realizing it, you repeat connections like someone who replays chapters even though they already know the ending.

Do you realize that love always hurts?

You will seek pain.

Do you tell yourself that you need to save others to feel valuable?

You will join those who need to be saved.

Do you think you can't ask for help?

You'll end up giving until you're empty.

And there you are. Confused, tired, frustrated.

Believing that life is punishing you. When in reality, you are obeying a story that doesn't belong to you. This chapter is for that: to look at how your personal narrative has shaped your relationships. And ask yourself: Am I loving from fullness or from fear? Am I allowing what I truly want or what fits my story of lack? Am I choosing consciously or repeating what I learned unknowingly?

You know that when you change your narrative, your way of loving also changes. And that change will not only improve your connections, it will also transform you from within.

Because you stop searching for love and start living it. From within you. Without effort. Without masks. Without emotional debt.

The projection of our stories in others
Every relationship you have is a stage where your internal narrative is projected without asking for permission. You're not just relating to the person in front of you. You are also relating to what you believe you deserve. With what you believe is love. With what you interpreted as care, abandonment, betrayal, or validation.

That's why it's no coincidence that you repeat patterns. You don't attract a "certain type of person"; rather, you attract experiences that fit your story.

If your narrative says "they leave me," you will resonate with someone who has one foot out the door.

If your narrative says, "I must always be strong," you will connect with someone who doesn't know how to support you.

If your narrative says, "I must earn love," you will end up with someone who makes you beg for it.

And no, it's not your fault. It's ignorance.

Because what you don't see, you repeat.

And what you don't heal, you project.

And what you don't question, you choose, over and over and over again... with different names.

Others are not your enemies. They are portals. Either they help you break your narrative or reinforce it. That's why, if you're in a relationship that hurts you, don't start by looking at the other person. Look at yourself.

What part of your story is holding it up?

And if you are in a relationship where you finally see yourself, hear yourself, feel free, ask yourself: What new part of me is starting to be written here?

Because when you change your story, the way you see the other person changes. You no longer need anyone to save you. Nor that they complete you. Nor make you feel valid.

You give yourself permission to love without emotional slavery. To let go without drama. Of staying without fear.

Others are mirrors. But you decide which part of you they reflect.

The effect of narrative on conflicts

Conflicts rarely begin with the facts. They start with the emotional interpretation of the facts. With the story you build in your head, before asking, before listening, before opening your heart.

"Surely he did it to hurt me."

"He wants to control me."

"He always acts like that because he doesn't respect me."

"I always end up being the one who gives in."

"I already knew this was going to happen."

The real conflict is often not outside. It's inside. And not because you made it up, but because your internal narrative was already loaded. And that emotional burden is what distorts the perspective.

Sometimes you don't fight with the person. You fight with your unresolved wound. With that feeling of abandonment you carry from before. With that need to be right to feel valuable. With that old idea that giving in is losing. With that fear of being invisible again.

When you don't review your narrative, you use conflict as a defense, not as a door. Defense to not feel, to not yield, to not expose yourself. And you call it dignity when many times it's wounded pride or unprocessed pain.

So, what happens when you decide to change the focus? You start to see conflict as a mirror. As an opportunity to review where you are reacting from.

You no longer attack. You ask.

You no longer run away. You name.

You no longer assume. You express yourself.

And that doesn't mean letting everything slide. It means inhabiting the conflict from the truth, not from the conditioned history.

When your narrative changes, the conflict is no longer a war. It's a conversation. A door. A reunion.

Rewriting shared narratives

Each relationship has a story. A kind of tacit script, sometimes unconscious, that both have been writing with silences, phrases, gestures, wounds, agreements, and customs.

And suddenly, one day you wake up in a dynamic that no longer represents you but that you continue living by inertia.

"He is always the strong one."

"She is always the one who explodes."

"I'm the one who keeps things in order."

"We don't talk about that."

"That's just how we are."

Those phrases uphold a shared narrative that becomes rigid, repetitive, and exhausting. What if you're no longer that character? And what if the other person isn't either?

What if that story you wrote together is no longer alive, but you keep acting it out?

Rewriting a shared narrative begins when someone dares to interrupt the pattern. Not with a complaint, but with a truth.

"I feel like we've been talking from the same place for years."

"I don't want to keep reacting like this with you."

"Can we rewrite this from who we are today and not from who we were?"

"I'm rediscovering myself, and I would like you to feel free to do the same."

Yes, it's uncomfortable. Yes, it's scary. Yes, sometimes the other person isn't ready. But if you are, it's already enough to change the tone of the story.

When one person in the relationship decides to speak from their present, even if the other still speaks from the past, something shifts. And sometimes that movement dismantles an old narrative that had already trapped them.

Rewriting together doesn't always mean staying together. But it does mean honoring each other along the way. Talk to each other from the current version. And not continue holding onto outdated roles.

When both give themselves permission to redraw, to evolve, to see each other with new eyes, the relationship does not get destroyed. It transforms, or it frees itself.

And both things are also love.

The power of stories in empathy

We all carry a story. Even the one who seems strong. Even the one who hurt you. Even you. And when you manage to remember that, something softens in you.

Empathy is not justifying the unjustifiable. It's understanding that many times the other is also acting from their own unaddressed wound.

The one who shouts may have been silenced. The one who leaves, perhaps, never learned to stay. The one who doesn't show love probably never received it as they needed. The one who betrays may not feel enough even for themselves.

That doesn't absolve them. But it does help you let go of the idea that everything revolves around you. Because sometimes, what hurts the most is not what the other person did, but the story you wove about it.

And when you can see the other without disguise, without loading them with your expectations, without demanding that they act from your script, that's where real empathy is born. Empathy that doesn't victimize. That doesn't idealize. That does not subjugate. But rather observes, recognizes, and chooses:

I know where you come from, but I also know where I stand. I don't need you to change for me to understand you, but I can decide whether I want to walk with you or not. I don't condemn you for what you did, but I also don't force myself to stay if it breaks me.

The power of stories in empathy lies in the fact that when you understand them, you stop fighting so much with others and start dialoguing with their pains.

And from there, you no longer react the same way. You no longer label so quickly. You no longer need to win the argument.

Because you know that sometimes, we are all telling a story to not give up. And that awareness gives you an unnegotiable peace.

CHAPTER 8

LIVE THE STORY YOU WANT TO TELL

Your life is the script;

live each day as if it were the most inspiring chapter.

We arrived here. And it wasn't by chance. This book was not just about reading, nor about understanding what happened to you, nor about reviewing the past. This book was a mirror. A sacred space to truly look at yourself. And now, right here, it's your turn to choose. Are you going to keep living the narrative you inherited, the one you fabricated to survive, or the story you can choose today from your truth?

Maybe your whole life revolved around what others expected of you. Maybe you stayed silent, complied, adapted. Maybe you were even successful, but inside something didn't add up.

And you felt tired, not because of what you did, but because of who you had to be to maintain it. Living the story you want to tell is stopping to survive. It's about stopping counting the days that pass and starting to inhabit the days you choose.

No, it's not about restarting everything. You don't need to leave your job, your friends, or your commitments. What you need is an internal, non-negotiable, radical decision. A decision that says:

From today, my decisions are aligned with my essence.

From today, every step I take carries my emotional signature.

From today, this new version belongs to me.

There is no more exhausting story than the one in which you cannot recognize yourself. And there's something that few say, but everyone feels. When you don't live the life you want to tell, your body shuts down, your eyes dim, and your soul hides.

But when you choose to live from your truth, even if it hurts, even if it challenges you, even if you lose things along the way, something in you ignites. And it doesn't go out anymore.

This chapter is not a closure. It's a door. And by crossing it, you are no longer asking for permission to be yourself. You are assuming the role that has always been yours: being the conscious author of your life.

Be the conscious author

Let me tell you something that no one tells you, but everyone should tattoo it: If you don't choose to write your story, someone else will do it for you.

And the worst part is that you won't even realize it. You're going to go through life repeating scenes that don't represent you, fulfilling expectations that don't matter to you, and accepting emotional crumbs as if they were banquets.

Because that's what happens when you live without narrative awareness.

You act, but you don't choose.

You react, but you don't decide.

You get up, work, eat, sleep, and one day you wake up in a life you didn't build. You just tolerated it.

Being a conscious author is not about writing what sounds good.

It's writing what resonates with you.

It's having the guts to look at the blank page and say: I'm writing this.

With my handwriting. With my truth. With who I am, even if I don't fit into what they expected of me.

And yes, it means losing people. It involves disappointing. It means that some will call you selfish, weird, intense, complicated.

But you know what? Worse is being lukewarm. It's worse to be what you're not just to fit into what you don't want. Choosing to be a conscious author is knowing that you can no longer blame the past.

You can no longer say, "I am this way because I was raised this way."

You can no longer repeat, "It's just that I've always been this way."

No.

That was the version without authorship. That was the copy. Now comes the original. And the original doesn't ask for approval. The original does not justify itself. The original does not live to please. This is a warning, not an inspiration:

If you decide to be the conscious author of your story, everything changes. From how you walk to who you share your bed with. From what you tolerate in a conversation to what you eat. There is no part of your life that is not affected by this choice.

So think it through. Because if you choose this, there's no turning back. And if you choose not to do it, that's valid too. But at least make it a decision, not an evasion.

Design your future through narrative

Designing the future doesn't mean having everything figured out. It's not about visualizing a perfect life nor creating a plan without room for error. Designing your future is something more intimate. More yours. It's sitting with yourself, in silence, and asking yourself with love:

"What story do I want to tell from now on?"

You don't need to know everything. You just need to be willing to write differently.

The narrative you live today is not an inevitable reflection of what happened. It's a starting point. And you decide if that point is a prison or a portal.

Every time you tell yourself "this no longer represents me," you are shaping something new. Every time you choose to think differently, even if your voice trembles, you are shaping the future with words that finally care for you.

It's not about changing the world all at once. It's about honoring your inner world. Maybe you can't change the story you lived. But you can change from where you remember it. And from that new place, you can create something different. Something softer. More free. More yours.

Designing your future through narrative is understanding that your internal story is the foundation of everything you build outside.

Your connections. Your decisions. Your limits. Your worth.

And that every word you choose to use with yourself can be a punishment or a bridge.

So today, just for today, choose to talk to yourself like someone who is learning to love themselves. Choose to write to yourself as someone who, at last, believes they deserve what they once only dreamed of.

And if tomorrow you doubt, if tomorrow your spirits fall, come back here. To this promise. To this beginning. To this design that is born from your deepest truth:

"My story doesn't end where I broke."

"My story is rebuilt every time I dare to believe that I can live something better and write it with my heart in my hand."

Evolve your narrative

You can't keep repeating the same old story and expect a different ending. And no, I don't mean what you say out loud. I mean what you tell yourself in silence.

When no one is watching.

When you look in the mirror.

When you sabotage yourself just before achieving it.

When you accept less than you are worth because "that's how it's always been."

That's the narrative you need to evolve. Not changing it for another equally false one, but prettier. Not decorating it with social media quotes.

Rather, evolve it. Level it up. Make her an adult. Real. Solid. Raw. Yours.

Do you want to know if your narrative has already expired?

Check if it limits you more than it frees you. Check if it is supported by fear, guilt, or the need for approval.

"I've always been like this."

"I'm not good at that."

"That kind of thing isn't for me."

"I don't work in relationships."

"I don't know how to let go."

They are phrases disguised as identity, but all they do is chain you to an old version of yourself.

Evolving your narrative is looking those phrases in the face and responding:

Maybe I was like that, but not anymore. Maybe before I didn't know how, but now I'm learning. Maybe I got hurt many times, but I no longer abandon myself.

Because you are not the wound. Nor the mistake. Nor the character you built to protect yourself. You are the version that is ready to be rewritten in real time. With awareness. With anger if necessary. With truth above all.

Do you want to evolve your story? Then stop repeating it from the place where it hurt. And start telling it from the place where you decided to heal. That's where the new begins. That's where the real begins. That's where you finally become the story you deserve to live.

Live your best version

Your best version is not perfect. It's not the most productive, nor the most admired, nor the one everyone understands.

Your best version is the most honest one.

The one that no longer makes excuses.

The one who knows when to move forward and when to stop.

The one who no longer pretends to be fine all the time. The one who dares to stay alone if necessary but never abandons herself again.

They have told you that your best version is a goal: the house, the body, success, the perfect partner. But what no one tells you is that your best version isn't seen... it's felt. You feel it when you take a deep breath and your chest doesn't hurt.

You feel it when you sleep peacefully, without pending conversations with yourself.

You feel it when you make decisions from peace, not from urgency.

You feel it when you don't need to convince anyone of who you are.

Simply, you are.

Living your best version is stopping surviving to fit in. It's choosing yourself even if you don't fit in. It's holding onto your truth even when everything else is shaking.

It's embracing yourself even on your broken days and not letting go of your hand.

And no, you're not always going to feel ready. But that doesn't matter. You don't need to be ready to start. You just need to be present.

Today I want you to say this out loud as a promise, as a pact: I didn't come to this life to replicate defeated versions of myself. I came to be free. I came to live from the root. I came to tell the story that has yet to be told: mine.

And every day that I choose consciously, I'm writing it.

The story we left behind

It's not enough to rewrite. You have to let it die. And you know it. You can't walk lightly carrying chapters that have already expired. You can't write a free life with the ink of your broken version.

And before you tell me that "it's hard to let go," let me warn you: The hard part is dragging along a story that no longer fits your skin.

If you really want to live differently, you have to bury who you were when you didn't know who you were. And that means looking at that history with love, yes, but also with firmness. Not to destroy it, but to thank it and let it go.

I was many things. I was the one who stayed silent, the one who pleased others, the one who postponed his truth out of fear of disappointing. I was the one who confused loyalty with sacrifice. The one who sought to be chosen, without understanding that the first vote was with myself.

I was also the one who hurt, the one who betrayed, the one who left, the one who broke. I was a version that needed to survive. And I don't judge her. I look at her. I hug her and leave her behind.

Today I recognize that I am no longer that story. That there is a new voice writing itself from within. A voice that doesn't explain itself; it stands firm.

Leaving behind is not forgetting. It's honoring from a distance. It's looking at that old chapter and saying: Thank you for bringing me this far. But from here on, I'm on my own. From here, I no longer need to act as if I don't know who I am.

Today I close this book knowing that the true ending is not in these pages. It's in what I decide after writing them. And that, that is truly mine. Completely mine. So, do it. Let go of that story with the courage of someone who finally understood that living is more important than understanding. The version of you that you were has already fulfilled its purpose. Now live it differently. Now make it worthwhile.

And you, who are reading this, what story are you going to leave behind? Because that decision, even if no one sees it, changes your soul.

FINAL THOUGHTS

What if I told you that this book wasn't about words? It was about wounds. About those that you hid so well that you didn't even remember they were still open. It was about silences. About those that scream in the early morning, when no one else is awake.

It was about you, about me, even though you tried to read it as if it were about someone else. Because you know that each line touched a corner you avoided looking at.

Each question was a crack. Each statement, a mirror. And each sentence, an invitation to stop lying to yourself. You don't have to say it out loud. But you know that at some point during this journey, you broke down. And not out of weakness. But because finally something inside you got fed up with pretending.

Pretend that you can do it alone.

Pretend that it doesn't hurt.

Pretend that everything is fine.

Pretend that you've already healed.

Pretend that you expect nothing from anyone.

Sometimes it's not that life breaks you. It's just that you were already broken, and finally something revealed it.

And that, even though it hurts, is the beginning of your freedom.

I was there too.

I also swallowed my emotions for years.

I also built a strong version of myself to not be weak in front of anyone.

I also convinced myself that love was sacrifice.

That being myself was going to cost me people. And I lost them. And I got lost. And I broke.

But here I am. With hands full of scars and a soul more alive than ever.

There's something that no one prepares you to feel: the grief of letting go of the story that held you.

That story that, although it hurt you, also gave you identity. It gave you a place in the world. An excuse. A coat. A narrative.

And now that you let it go, you feel naked. Alone. Exposed.

But, you know what? That's how real life begins. You don't have to be strong now. You just have to be honest.

Tell your story what you never told it:

"Thank you for bringing me this far, but I no longer need you."

"Thank you for protecting me, but now I can stand on my own with my truth."

"Thank you for everything, and sorry for so much."

And then he cries. Don't stop. Don't wipe your face so quickly. Let that salty water bring out what has been stuck for centuries. Don't explain it. Don't rationalize it. Just let it out.

Because when you finish crying, you'll notice something. Something subtle, small but eternal.

You are no longer the same. And there's no going back.

This book never tried to teach you anything. It only came to remind you of what you already knew. But you had forgotten, buried, or denied it to survive.

No longer survive. Live, love, rewrite, reinvent yourself, reconcile with the chaos, and never let anyone write your story again without your permission.

And if at any moment you feel lonely again, come back to these pages.

Here you will always find yourself.

Here you will always return to yourself.

Because this story is yours. And you're still in time to turn it into the most fucking beautiful one you've ever lived.

The science behind your inner story

If you've made it this far, it's because something inside you has already changed. And for that change not to remain just in emotions but to be sustained in consciousness and real power, you need to know something: your story doesn't just live in your mind; it lives in your body. And science confirms it.

1. *Your narrative is neurobiology*

Every thought you repeat, every story you recreate, literally modifies your brain. This is called neuroplasticity. Your brain is capable of reorganizing itself based on your repeated experiences. Every time you repeat "I'm not enough," you reinforce a neural network that automates that belief. Every time you choose a new, more realistic thought, you create a new path.

This is not magic.

It's biology.

Your mind does not distinguish between what you imagine and what you live. That's why your narrative has the power to shape your physical and emotional identity.

2. *Your history somatizes*

Did you know that 80% of the signals in the nervous system travel from the body to the brain (and not the other way around)?

This means that your body influences your mind more than your mind influences your body.

The emotions you don't express, the stories you don't let go of, are stored in tissues, organs, and breathing.

That's why there are pains that have no medical cause but do have an emotional root. And when you decide to rewrite your story, your body also starts to heal.

3. Your psychological defense system doesn't sabotage you; it protects you.

The brain is designed to seek security, not happiness. That's why you repeat patterns. That's why you react the same way even though "you already know." That's why it's hard for you to change even when you want to. It's not laziness. It's not weakness. It's protection.

Your limbic system (where emotion, memory, and fear reside) blocks abrupt changes if it senses a threat. But when you give it new safe experiences, new sustained narratives, your brain understands: "I no longer need to protect myself from this."

And there, yes… it frees you.

4. The power is in body awareness

It's not enough to think differently. You have to feel differently. Changing your story means feeling it in your body. Breathe differently. Move differently. Relate from new sensations.

Implicit memory (the one that lives in your body) only transforms through real emotional experiences.

That's why you cried.

That's why you trembled.

That's why you felt heat, anger, relief.

Your body was rewriting itself with you.

And now where does this leave you? It leaves you in a place of power. Because you no longer depend on the past, your environment, or what others expect.

Understanding how you function is the key to stop judging yourself and start designing yourself. You are neuroplasticity. You are a living experience. You are body, emotion, mind, and will.

Now you know that your story can hurt, but it doesn't have to condemn you. It can mark you, but it doesn't have to limit you. It may have been written from trauma, but it can be rewritten from awareness.

And that is true power. Not the power to change everything all at once. But rather the recognition that you can start anew every day. And do it from the most real place that exists: the one you chose.

Thank you for making it this far.

See you where new stories are born.